Wraith Like Me

A Poetry Collection

Geneva Oleander

Contents

Dedication

For every little girl who ever dreamed of growing up to be a real poet,
here's the big secret:
you were *always* a real poet.

Author's Forward

I wrote the oldest of these poems fifteen years ago, and I wrote the bulk of these poems over the last ten years. One may wonder why I've been hoarding poems like a dragon with a far less shiny trove, and the answer is far less exciting than one Smaug may give you. It is not greed that has kept many of these poems in the depths of my computer, but rather, the fear of hurting those who have hurt me.

There is an Anne Lamott quote I have shared with all of my creative writing students over the last decade that goes, "You own everything that happened to you. Tell your stories. If people wanted you to write warmly about them, they should have behaved better." I share this quote without hesitation in an effort to help my students find their voice and their courage in telling their stories. It always sparks discussion and a little debate, but it almost always leads the class to agree that you own what happened to you and that you are allowed to share those stories. And yet, despite the fact that I now write under a pseudonym for a variety of reasons, I have feared sharing some of the things people did to me for fear of hurting them. It has taken a lot of growth and courage to share these poems with you here now, but I think it's finally time they find their feet in this strange world of ours.

So, I share these poems today with a few caveats.

Firstly, I don't name anyone in these poems. I have changed names and a few details in very specific poems in an effort to spare a few people in my life who would be painstakingly obvious to anyone who knew us. While I think I have done a good job of it, I am only human. If you think you find yourself in one of these poems and you do not like how you are presented, remember that our truths are a personal thing. I am sure I am the villain in someone's story. I have tried very hard to live a life of compassion and love, but I am confident I have fucked it up a time or two. I welcome you to write your own poems about me because I truly think poetry is an integral part of the healing process.

Secondly, not every poem is strictly autobiographical (though every poem here has truth in it). Some of these poems told from "she" or "he" perspectives are about family members or friends who shaped my life, whose stories I shared in as anonymous a fashion as I could. My opinion or understanding of anyone else's truth is certainly a very subjective interpretation. I think that too is something beautiful about poetry and art—the subjectivity in the making and the interpretation by the audience (readers, viewers, etc.) is what makes it so special.

Thirdly, I firmly believe there are only a few people in my life who could sift through these poems to figure out which poem is about which lover and which time in my life. Like many children who did not see the best example of a happy, healthy marriage in my childhood home, I often sought solace in the arms of people who did not know how to show love in a way that was kind and thoughtful. It took me a long time to realize that everything I thought I knew about love was wrong, and I hope some of those lessons can be imparted here for anyone who cares to hear them. I didn't write these poems as an ode to all my shitty exes, but really, as a reminder that imperfect, hurting people (myself included) make imperfect, painful relationships. I am a better partner because I took time to heal and grow before I became a wife and mother.

Fourthly, I believe people can grow and change. I am not who I was fifteen years ago, and while my college boyfriend will forever be twenty-three (the age he was when we broke up) in my memories, I like to believe he is someone less toxic now. I sure hope that who he is in these poems and in my memories is not who he remained forever. The same goes for the poems I have written about my childhood. People grow up. A divorce can make people happier, better versions of themselves. I've seen it happen to the people I love most in this world. Read these poems and enjoy them as the art form they are. Please do not use them as character witnesses against anyone we know in real life.

In that same vein, the truths I share in these poems are often no longer true for me. There were times when I thought I could never love again or could never love anyone like my childhood best friend, high school sweetheart (etc. etc.), and I was wrong. Please don't hold those truths against me either. I changed too. I'm sure the truths from my newest poems might look different when the next book of poems comes out in five years too. Truth is not only subjective to each person, it is subjective to that precise moment in time. Truth and reality are sticky subjects that cannot be pinned down for very long. I strongly believe that as an artist, especially when we are talking about emotions.

This fifth and final caveat is more of a reminder: you are enough, and (in the same token) you will never be too much for the right chosen family and the person who will choose you every day. I wish

I had known that fifteen years ago. I wish I had known that before I spent way too many years trying to make myself smaller, quieter, prettier, thinner, etc. etc. And while I have you here—love should not hurt. It does not leave marks. It does not scream or yell or slam doors. Love does not force you or beg you to do things you are uncomfortable with. Love is gentle and kind. Love is soft. It is a springtime morning, *not* a hurricane. If I could tell my eighteen-year-old self anything, it might just be, "Everything you think you know about love is wrong."

I hope you enjoy the little bits of me pressed between these pages. My poetic style has changed over the years, and even now, I find myself breaking conventions and playing with rules in every poem I write. One of the things that has stayed the most consistent is my love of titles. They are an essential part of the poem, and I really encourage everyone to read into them when they read my poem (and some likely have to be Googled). My husband prefers to read the poem first and then Google the title, but the order is up to you! If you're a fellow rulebreaker and convention bender, you just might love these poems too!

Content Warnings

This book contains references to physical, sexual, and emotional violence, miscarriage, suicide, and mental illness. This is my lived experience, but if it is too hard for you to interact with, I strongly encourage you against reading these poems.

To my father—

WHO LEFT HIS PREGNANT, 15-YEAR-OLD GIRLFRIEND—

it was easy to hate
you for leaving us,
easier yet to forgive.

The Saturday Morning After He Hit Her

the window was open,
the curtains blew in the breeze,
and all she left behind were the feathers
loosed free from her wings.

Monster

A knock on the door.
A creak.
An entrance.
A closed door.
Heavy breathing.
No need for lights.
No monster beneath the bed.
No ghosts in the closet.
Checking is just for show.
A reason is the only reason for the looking.
A weight on the bed.
A shuffling of sheets.
No monsters beneath the bed—
but rather, one atop it.

Growth

Somehow it feels like my mother simultaneously never grew up and grew up too quickly. She was thrown into adulthood, headfirst. There was no growing, only showing up the first day as a woman without realizing she'd seen her last day as a child, and I can't help but wonder who she would have been if she'd been allowed to grow slowly through relationships and adventures, through heartbreaks and failures and successes. If she too had made it to thirty without children and a mortgage, would the world be different, bettered by her undivided attention?

What if being my mother stunted her growth?

Pebble Road

was between your house and mine
  it wasn't exactly the middle, it was at least a block closer to mine,
but it meant something to have sacred ground between us
it meant something to stand there waiting for you to meet me on the
stony stretch of ground that only SUV's drove through unharmed
it meant something to have our own Terabithia on a stretch of rock
protected by curling, hugging, ancient pines-
it meant something to us

when I think about your mom's cancer I remember a softball field-
she called my parents over and whispered to them while you told me
what the secret was
and I cried unabashedly because it didn't make any sense and I didn't
want her to die,
I didn't want you to hurt, and I didn't want Pebble Road, the few
blocks between your house and mine, the giggles during endless sum-
mer sleepovers,

or anything else–
to change

she got too sick to stay at home and you came to live with us
Pebble Road was still something magical,
some place we walked to remember what it was like before
and we walked so much that spring, walked miles and miles of mem-
orized ground until our feet knew the asphalt better than our eyes—

but we couldn't walk away
from her death

she died on Ash Wednesday
it only matters because we were both Catholic then and we've both
spent a decade
falling
in and out of God
you say you've finally found him while I'm still wandering,
but no amount of searching can take us back to Pebble Road
we walk along the rocks when we make it back home but it's not the
same road
the years we spent running away from that place eroded away what it
meant
to two little girls
who thought cancer was something that happened to old people,
death was something that happened to grandparents,
and we were a five minute walk away from each other
not a $500 plane ride over 2,500 miles of distance

and maybe it doesn't matter what came next

maybe it doesn't matter that you moved away to Georgia, then California

and I ran away to college and lied about where I was from

maybe it doesn't matter that home isn't two blocks away from Pebble Road anymore-

maybe all that matters is we had a Pebble Road and that once upon a time, it meant something

Confession

"My child, have you sinned since we last spoke?" *We've never spoken.*
This is my first confession "Um...I think so." He waited for me to
elaborate. *Sins? I kissed Jordan last summer, and I told Kyle my bra*
size. Are those sins? I didn't have sex with either of them. Do I have to
bring it up? Shit. He's just waiting for me to speak. Is cursing in my
thoughts a sin? Maybe I could ask him to list all the sins and then I
could take it from there. "Grace?" He spoke my name. This was no
confession booth. This was a small room with two chairs, a crucifix,
a Bible, a priest, and a fourteen-year-old girl who didn't really get the
whole confession thing. "I was mean to someone..." I finally said. *Who*
the hell was I mean to? Maybe I could just tell him that was a lie so that
then I have a sin to confess. "Go on." He said. "I bullied this boy on the
bus." *I don't even ride the bus. I walk to school.* "I made him cry, and I
felt bad about it." *I have never made anyone cry.* There was a simple
admonishment, words lost to time and then—"Let us say a Hail Mary
together. Think of your sins while we pray. Tell yourself why we must
love all of God's children."

"Hail Mary, full of grace.
The lord is with thee.
Blessed art thou amongst women,
and blessed is the fruit of thy womb,
Jesus.

Holy Mary, Mother of God,
pray for us sinners,
now and at the hour of our death.
Amen."

The *amen* hangs in the air between us when we finish, and I wonder
if he knows this first confession will be my last confession.

Raging Waters

Seizing

Clenching

Pain

A memory wraps itself around me like the long spiked tail of some great beast of legend

Some monster from another world

Barbed

Venomous

A scream roaring through my veins

A black river coursing through the arteries of my heart

Squeezing its monstrous black waves through too small holes in once mighty rock

Shaping them, shaping me, into something in its own reflection

Hollowing me out

Emptying me

Leaving a shell of someone who used to be great, or might have been great if the darkness did not swallow me

A voice in my head
A small dangerous hope
Do I get to come back from this?
Only the sound of raging water answers.

Savage

In some alternate universe
  do I get to be the girl who was not broken,
do I get to grow up to be a woman who does not shudder when the
conversation turns
who needs content warnings and trigger warnings to read books,
watch movies–to exist,
who lives my life leaping between bouts of darkness

in some alternate universe
do I end up as someone else entirely if I never meet him
if I never trust him
if I never let myself be alone with him–
do I still get to be *me* without his savagery?

Fire

I was only looking for flowers.
I was only looking for flowers.
And you,
you
burned the entire fucking forest to the ground.

Justice

Years after you carved me up and left my wounds to fester
 I tried to find you
Facebook. Twitter. Google.
It was like you disappeared
like the monster in my nightmares had been wiped off the face of the
Earth–
And so in my fantasies, my deepest, darkest hopes,
I told myself that somewhere between your crimes against me and that
internet search
your heart stopped beating, that you bled out somewhere
a dark, evil life snuffed out too late
and sometimes, it feels like justice
like the reparations no court in this country would ever give me
come to me when I imagine you incapable of hurting
someone else like you hurt me

Justice

such a loaded word
hard to talk around like a mouth full of rocks
or the memory of your hands on my body–
and if you're not rotting in the ground somewhere
I don't want to know, I don't want to know that you got to live a
normal life devoid of the haunting you left inside me

I realize
not finding you that day was a mercy
and if I never look again,
I can continue to live with the possibility that maybe, *maybe*
you're truly gone from this world
and you can never hurt me again

Mia

Goddammit, Mia, we were never good at small talk. We were good at kissing beneath the covers and lying to our parents. We were good at fooling everyone, including ourselves. But we were never good at small talk.

We were fantastic at breakfast. We could get away with it the morning after because no one knew it was the morning after. We were best friends—young and innocent; and *lesbian* and *bisexual* weren't words our parents even thought about. Breakfast was always the best—do you remember the smoked sausages your mom always bought? Little Smokies—I called them teeny wieners, and we'd laughed because neither of us knew what a real dick looked like, and it seemed funny back then.

We were the worst at breaking up, did we even break up? Or did we just pretend it never happened and start dating boys? I don't even know. I can't even remember. I do remember finally fucking my first boyfriend on a cloudy night. I remember rushing back to you—you held me and told me you loved me. I didn't ask you what that meant, but the next day we went back to our lives and tried not to remember what it felt to be in the right place together.

We were great together. I remember that. I remember falling in and out of love with you for over a decade and I remember the day I decided I couldn't do it anymore. I packed up my life and moved four hours away. You tried to call, tried to act like a protective girlfriend but you weren't and we weren't.

Now we're in this place, this smoky bar and you're trying to rekindle something that was never even allowed to blaze. A fire can't hide away for six years then just burst into flames again; that's just not how love works. You want to know if I'm going to settle down with some guy and start a family like I'm supposed to. You know I am, of course I am, but I have amnesia when I'm around you. Goddammit, Mia, we're not good at small talk, and we're even worse at lying to each other.

Blue Planet

paint on an orb of clay stretched and kicked into a world alive
swirl the whites, make it abstract and call it art
watch from afar as the invisible painter paints little drops of humans
beneath the more beautiful strokes of brush on canvas
watch and wonder why we are alive and the moon is dead
when the same painter painted us both into existence
(and then tell me why he painted the rocks first) ?

Sapayoas

we spent our lives in awe
  of those who pioneered ahead,
of those who weren't afraid,
those who took the steps
we were too afraid to take

you and I were only girls
and they say girls are never brave
though we aren't so old these days,
the world was different then,
we decided to cast aside our swords,
to fight one less battle in our war-locked lives

we were of the quiet *b*,
the ones who didn't have to lie to love a man,
and maybe it didn't make us lucky,
but we did get to pick and choose

and that was the reason,
yes that was the reason
I failed to choose you.

Books

I seek solace in
education because it's
the love of my life
when I say this, you
look away, because you thought I
loved you more than books.

Born Anxious

You don't know what it's like.
  It's not just sweaty palms
and a fluttering heart,
It's more than the words you read
in the library to try to understand
what it's like to sit in my skin
day in and day out.

It's like someone erected a shopping mall
in the meadow behind my childhood home.
I remember running through the tall grass
when I was kid, laughing with the butterflies,
I remember my first bee sting
and the tobacco my mother pulled out the front
of a new Virginia Slim and pressed on my leg
to draw the stinger out.
And even now standing between Victoria's Secret

and Old Navy,
with a wailing child to my right
and three teenagers with pockets full of stolen merchandise
to my left—I can feel the sting,
still smell the earth stuck to my feet
and the tobacco wet with spit pressed to my skin.

It's being a stranger in my own mind
I remember what it was like to possess
this terrain,
to be sovereign of this realm—
or maybe I don't.
Maybe I created this memory to convince myself
that I was normal once
that there was a time before Chaos
stole my crown and whirled away
singing in a language I'd forgotten how to speak.

And then there is the clutter–
the clutter keeps me awake at night.
There is a place for everything I own
a place I designated specifically to hold it
but there is no shelf for thoughts,
there is no order to the Fear that has eloped
with Eris and co-governs the
meadow-mall I used to love.

I don't even know what is real anymore.
Is it what I think or what I don't?
What I know or what I fear?

It's more than loss of appetite
and decreased concentration,
more than anything you'll find
written by a doctor who sees
people like me.
No study would ever say that
it's losing control of the very thing
that separates humans from beasts.

I Forgive You

hate is a flame, fire
that consumes all in its path
leaving only ash

The Runner

Little legs pumping
running away from another fight
slamming doors
ripping cords
run, run, running
There was also so much running
a running that didn't end when the cops came
or when the apologies poured around us like
the kind of honey that stuck to everything
uncomfortable and hard to scrub off

a running that carried me through years of
reading about girls who got to escape,
biding my time until a letter came to carry me away
there were no castle, but goddammit–
Burress Hall sure looked like one
and college was full of boys who swore they were men

there was kisses and moonlight and D.C. money
–it felt like maybe I could run towards something–
if I could swallow down all the parts of me he couldn't digest

but the slamming doors started
a broken wrist, drinking, yelling–
So much yelling,□
apologies that didn't even try to be sweet
hollow and putrid
the kind of apologies that made me miss
the stickiness of honey

finally–
a retreat to the running shoes of my childhood.
he told me I was making a mistake,
that running was going to be the regret of my life
How many times did he remind me I had nothing?
But he had everything
Money, money, *money*–
the money wasn't enough to stop me from running away
from the gilded version of the cage I grew up in

legs, longer now–
run, run, running
until somewhere, someone who felt like
springtime just might give me a reason to sit,
to stay, *to be*–
to feel safe enough to stretch bare toes out in the grass
and nap awhile in the warmth of the sun
and let my heart rate rest, my muscles relax,

and for once my miserable life, *feel safe*.

Unworthy

It's funny that your father, the doctor, always treated me like I wasn't
worthy of you. I was too poor, too un-serious, too unworthy in all
the ways he thought mattered most. Ironic that of the two of us–me
and you–only one of us ended up a doctor in the end–
and it wasn't you.

Lost Time

you met me on the battlefield wearing skinny jeans and converse,
you marveled at my armor, my broadsword, my horse, my power
I was strength personified, a warrior fighting for a better world
but your vulnerability enticed me, called me, spoke to me, tricked
me.
your smile and your long legs set me burning
until my only option was to climb down from my horse
and let you strip me of my armor and make love me to me atop the
blood of my enemies.
I let you cast my sword aside because you made me feel safe,
and I realized too late that this was all an enemy plot
to tear down a warrior,
to strip me of my weapons and my strength
so you could create a damsel where a soldier once had been
you took pleasure in deconstructing the life I created for myself.
you only dated warriors because breaking us made you feel strong.

I wish someone would have told me that loving you meant I could never return to battle-

or at least, I couldn't return so long as I loved you and it would take years to remake myself into the champion I was before you. Think of all the battles I could have waged, all the wars I could have won, if I had never met you.

Wild Things

I am a lioness, feral and wild, all teeth and claws and hunger
you keep me close because I'm beautiful and interesting,
a magnificent beast to show off to your friends
they marvel at how tame I am,
congratulate you on beating the wildness out of me
you accept their compliments but you keep your eyes on me
you don't show your fear but I can smell it
we both know I am not tame
wild things never break
we bend, we play along but our charm is the danger
our allure is the unpredictable
sometimes you see the longing in my eyes
you see me daydreaming of the open savannah
feel me missing the hunt
and that's why you want me,
that's why you love me—

    you know at any moment I might drop the charade

and rip your fucking heart out

One for the Road

I knock on the door of Apartment 410A. In two years of sharing this apartment with him, I'd never knocked before. He comes to the door with a painted-on smile: "Your stuff is right in here." I follow him wordlessly. The walls are bare without me, the bookshelf empty. My voice breaks the heartache, nearly-tangible, enveloping us like a shirt that doesn't fit (it had grown too big for us): "It looks so different in here." He falters: "I'm moving when the lease is up. It's too full of memories." We stumble, trip, fall across the room into each other's empty arms. There is urgency in our kisses, longing in our lovemaking. There are tears as we pull our clothes back on. He breaks: "Does this mean—" I stand firm: "It's still over. I love you, but we both know it's never going to work." I grab the final box of my things, the final proof that we had spent four years trying to make this love work. I remember the Christmas we spent in San Diego, the road trip to Albuquerque, the hours spent studying together, the house we wanted to build in Arizona, the life we'd dreamed up so clearly for ourselves that it too felt like a memory, the children we'd never have together (a boy named

Owen and a girl named Selene)— "This is for the best, even if it doesn't feel like it now." I open the door, look back into the world I'd never know again. He leans in close: "One for the road?" I nod. One long kiss and it's all over. I close the door behind me and walk on.

Who Left You Here to Die?

Your blue eyes remind me of my grandmother,
  remind me of myself and I find myself looking
into them, trying to figure out who left you here to die.
I imagine you young and healthy,
I imagine you lying next to the man your mother said
wasn't good enough for you,
the moonlight dancing through the window on your pale skin
illuminating the smile on your sleeping face.
And then you're married in my mind,
married to the man from the moonlit evenings.
You're scaling the Himalayas, swimming in the Caribbean,
living like you knew you'd end up here
with numbered days and only memories to sustain you.
I imagine you doing all the things I haven't gotten around to yet,
all the dreams I've saved for the future.

And the man you loved, your husband, must have died on some
foreign battlefield or from a disease far longer and uglier.
I try to understand what it must have felt like to lose him
before you had children or maybe after years of trying without suc-
cess—
worse yet, I imagine you raising your children, loving them
and being the best mother you could be only for them to abandon you
now.
I smile in the rearview mirror as I drive you across town for dialysis
every Wednesday and Friday and try to pretend I'm not writing your
life in my head,
not trying to convince myself you lived every moment of your life
with the fullness it deserved,
not trying to understand what kind of family left you here to die.

The Screaming Man

I am on the edge of everything
  but still a slave to my restlessness,
slave to my passport,
always scanning the horizon for
home.

You will never be free
He says, cigarette between his teeth—
you will always be moving,□
always be reaching.
Your wanderlust is a curse.

Standing alone on the deck of a ship
headed for tomorrow,
and I am Munch's screaming man.
For those like us there can be no peace,
there can be no *home*.

Restlessness

All the times my father told me that I could be anything I wanted to be when I grew up, we always seemed to be sitting on our front porch, fretting over bills and a mortgage my parents could never really afford. He would tell me that I could dream as big as I wanted to, that my brain and my work ethic would carry me far beyond the boundaries of the town that I grew up in, the town that trapped him. I could always see him playing my future in his head, just behind his eyes—golden and star-studded, he must have imagined I'd be wealthy and happy, that I would succeed where he failed, that I would wake up every morning without a worry in my heart.

He taught me more life lessons than I can fit on this page. He taught me how to throw a softball, how to successfully cram for a test, how to swim, how to read, how to impress a potential employer—but he never taught me how to just *be*—probably because he never learned that trick himself. So I spent my life running from the low expectations strangers set for me when they realized my parents were children when they brought me into this world, always running toward the shock on those same people's faces when I did it better than the kids always destined for greatness, the ones who grew up on the other side of town.

I dream. I reach. I work until I'm not sure I have any work left in me and then I work some more. I achieve—but I never mastered reveling in the warmth of my success. When you spend your life dreaming of being the best, nothing ever really seems to be enough. There is always more money to be made, more things to be had, more degrees to be earned.

I often find myself restless, my wild heart beating against my chest—thump, thump, thumping against the body that cages it—dreaming of catching the next plane out of town headed anywhere but here, wondering what it would really be like in a new place every year, reaching for my passport to teach me lessons I cannot find in a book, lost in the insatiability that has accompanied me like a friend through all of my days.

This restlessness is more than wanderlust, it's more like the innate desire to always be more than I am in this moment. There will always be another graduate degree, another honor to put behind my name—there will always be some better, more accomplished version of myself just waiting for me to grow into her.

This discontent, this restlessness swims through my veins like a disease, sometimes dormant for weeks or months until I think I might actually be happy, that this *me* might actually be enough—but then the disease flares up again and hangs around my neck like a noose, my contentedness recedes and I am left reaching and hoping—fearing that I may never learn how to wake up in the morning, look out my window at a beautiful sky painted vibrant hues of blue and think, *This—this—this life, this moment, this* me *is good enough.*

And until that morning rises with the sun—or maybe *if* that morning ever rises with the sun—I must keep racing toward a finish line that is always moving further away from me, hoping that one day my wild, untamed heart will learn how to wear a saddle.

Dido

broke all the glasses in the cabinet
after you hung up,
threw them to the ground and watched them shatter
glass splattered
across the hard wood floors
thought of lying down,
pressing my face against the shards
if only to remember
I had a beating heart
as the blood pooled against my skin
a reminder I didn't get to die
when you stopped loving me

Future

the future fades away
like black and white memories;
if I believed it, if I saw it and I dreamed it,
is losing it something I can mourn?

Unafraid

I have spent the last fourteen years looking for you in every man who
touches me,
in every woman who kisses me.
I have closed my eyes and felt you,
dreamed up a different future while making plans for the reality I am
stuck in.
I have been waiting for you to show up on my doorstep,
heart in your hand and plans in your head.
I have been waiting for a moment that came and went when we were
children playing at love and lovemaking,
girls who didn't know that our love for one another somehow affected
our heterosexuality,
girls who thought our fingers inside of one another, our tongues inside
of one another
was a rite of passage, something all girls did.
I have been passively waiting all these years for you to realize you're in
love with me

while I hide my own love in a box deep inside of me,

a box half-memory, half-dream

and I am tired of living my life afraid to tell you that I didn't stop loving you when we decided it was time we stopped wasting our time with each other and start loving men.

I didn't stop loving you when I loved other people, when I moved in and shared a bed with other people, built a life with other people,

and I don't think I'll stop loving you when I settle down with the wrong person

because telling you I love you might mean I lose our friendship,

and our friendship is the last relic of a love I was too stupid to hold onto when it was all around me, the final black and white photograph of who we were and who we could have been

if we had lived our lives unafraid.

Less Blue

it used to be easier to stay,
 easier to fake contentedness
but it didn't fit, couldn't fit—

it was bending the edge of a sky piece
and shoving it into the half-constructed ocean
puzzles don't work that way
and once the bit of sky
was smashed, shoved, molded into
something it wasn't meant for—
it was useless

there was nothing left to do
but throw it out
and tell his friends he'd lost the piece
or maybe it was broken when he got it—
defective, unfixable

better, maybe, just to start a
new puzzle—
an easier one with less blue

Expiration Date

Everyone should love someone with
an expiration date in mind.
An abstract date or actual end date,
everyone should know what it's like to love someone
who's already half-way out the door.
One foot planted firmly in your life,
the other poised, ready to run.

It's better than the one night stand where all your passion
is used up like the month's rent money the first Friday night
after payday.
And it's different than the kind of love that follows you
through all the seasons of your life.
Every moment is fleeting, every embrace already half-shadow,
there is fear and there is lamentable hope sewn into the seams.

Loving with your eye on the exit sign above the door

is freedom in chains.

It is running into the burning building while everyone around you
begs you to save yourself while there's still time.

But there is only purgatory for those living with the *what ifs*
there is no salvation for those that do not seek damnation.

You cannot be saved if you lived your life in the shade.

Everyone should love someone with
an expiration date in mind.

Love them quickly,

drink in too much of them before everything is spoiled,

and when there is nothing left but moldy drops in the bottom of the
pail,

let them go with the sweetest goodbye you can muster.

Nienna

I remember how badly I wanted to be your wife
I thought if you could just heal from your parents late-in-life divorce,
the hollowing out of your trust in monogamy,
perhaps we could cross the bridge that lay between us
I thought that was the pressing issue that prevented us
from closing that distance and making that commitment
but now that I am someone else's wife,
someone who does not constantly disappoint me,
I can't imagine what would have happened
if we actually jumped that gulf together.

I hope you healed
I truly do,
but I am so glad you didn't fix your shit
while I was still sharing your bed.

Nomadic

If it hurts to leave, don't leave.□

My father's words play in my head
on repeat,
I hit shuffle but the same warnings
pop up again and again;
this playlist is the only one
I've downloaded.

It's not too late to change your mind,□
you don't have to go.

My defense seems weak,
if we were in court,
he could rest his case,
case closed,
the prosecution would be awarded the key

to my chains—
but luckily for me,
I am judge, jury, and lawman
in my own comings and goings.

Are you running away from here,☐
or are you running toward there?

I wish it didn't matter that I can't
make him understand,
I keep trying because I want him
to know why I have to go,
why I have to move 1,000 miles away
from everything I know.
I want him to know that I never had a choice,
the city called me away,
it enchanted me,
and I don't want to break the spell.

Your brother is like me, he wants to sleep in the same bed☐
with the same woman in the same house his entire life.

I want him to see himself when he looks at me
but I can't do that at the expense of
my own happiness,
and even if I am always reaching,
always moving,
even if I was born nomadic
with one foot always in this place and the next,
even then,

I know no other way of living,
no other way of being.

I'm behind you though. Even if I don't get it,□
I support you 100%. I promise.

And even though it hurts to leave,
even though my heart is broken
by the going,
it doesn't mean that I am wrong,
It doesn't mean that I should stay.

Lies we tell before bed

As the move draws closer, we find ourselves lost in conversation every night before we turn off the light. We tell each other that one day we will find ourselves in the same place at the same time. We pretend that our inability to be happy in the same geographical location is the only issue we face; we say distance is the true tragedy of our love. We talk about tomorrow like it's not already gone. We lament how unfair, how cruel it is that I'll be there and you'll be here. We pretend that we aren't both dreaming of our freedom. And it's easier to tell people that we loved each other but logistics got in the way, easier than admitting that even with hearts full of love for one another, we could never work.

And maybe that is the real tragedy here: somehow we are wired differently. We are innately wrong for each other. There is no blame to go around, no fingers to be pointed. We can't pen a list of grievances and leave them on the pillow for the other to find.

We just don't fit.

It's as simple, as complicated, as cruel as that.

A Question

A question.

"But New Orleans is so far. Why do you have to move?"

An answer.

"You never asked me to stay."

New Orleans

You came into sight as I drove across the Mississippi River. Dark and mysterious, I'd followed your voice over 858 miles of open road. Your call, like a siren's song in the night, beckoned me closer. They warned me about your dark magic. They warned me about your voodoo and the dark spirits that danced between your thighs. They told me to cling to my non-beliefs, to arm myself with the knowledge that your magic wasn't real. It was all illusion, a trick of the light and the bourbon and the heat.

But no one warned me about your softer side. While I was looking for ghosts, you slipped a love potion in my drink. You came to me that first night with eyes as wild and as dark as your hair. When you kissed me, you tasted like danger but you spoke of adventure. Your beads jingled when you danced for me, and I sat in reverence as you lit spirit candles and read my future in your cards.

All roads, you said, *lead you back to me.*

I left you on a Saturday. I watched you disappear beyond the waters as I drove away. Your wild hair, your inviting hips, your long, dark fingers begged me to return. You played your best saxophone solo and called down soft rains to cool the boiling streets. You filled the air with the scent of po' boys and gumbo—and all the while, you called my name across the river, pleading with me to turn my car around. You promised me that I'd never wake up in a fog of discontent if I stayed, promised I'd never be bored again. You asked me to remember the way we'd danced in the street and the way I'd laughed as you kissed powdered sugar off my lips in Café du Monde. *Remember*, I whispered, *as if I could forget a single moment with you.*

I pushed the pedal to the floor. On the other side of the bridge, I rolled down the window and yelled back the promises I'd made you the last night we'd danced beneath the street lights—*I will come back to you. I will come back, and I will never leave.*□

First appeared in Belle Rêve Literary Journal

The Water-Logged Heart

(Or, Banksy's New Orleans' Girl)

If her dress were purple and her cheeks were pink, if
a smile curled the edges of her plump lips, if
she held a book or a violin or a baseball glove, if
her face wasn't full of what she'd seen, if
she believed that the rain would stop, if
she was laughing or dancing or singing, if
she didn't look half-drowned, all-wild, if
she were any other girl on any other building—
—she wouldn't belong to us.

*First appeared in r.kv.r.y Quarterly Literary Magazine in April 2016

Hurricane Season

You ask me if I love you. You ask me after sex which always cheapens anything I say. You ask me if I love you, and I start to think about the weather—about the nature of storms and men and anger and passion and love and forgiveness and relationships. And I try not to tell you that you are a soft rain that falls on a warm morning in June, you are the sprinkling rain that cools off my skin before the sun comes out and a pleasant, cool breeze leaves a lovely, calm day. You are comfort and you are safe and you are reliable—but you are only a warm day in June. I try not to tell you that I have loved hurricanes—storms that tore through my life and flooded my soul, possessed my body and carried me away with their howling winds. Hurricanes that wrecked my life, my home, and my mind. Hurricanes that left only devastation and longing in their wake.

And maybe I'm a storm chaser, an adrenaline junkie who doesn't know a good man when he is lying next to her, asking her if she loves him because he loves her desperately, because he doesn't know how he'll breathe if she tells him no. And maybe I don't know how to be a normal woman with a normal husband who works a 9 to 5 job with a cookie cutter house and a few cookie cutter kids—maybe I'm just wired wrong. Maybe there's a glitch in my system, and one day I'll drown after the hurricanes have come and gone and swallowed me up in their flood waters. Maybe all of that is true, but I can't lie to you another moment. So when you ask me if I love you, I'm going to look into your eyes and tell you I love you like a warm day in June. And when you ask me what that means, I'm going to tell you—"I don't know" because really, I don't know.

Odysseus, King of Night

I am Odysseus, lost at sea, always scanning the horizon for home,
twenty years seems like twenty lifetimes
and I am paralyzed with homesickness.

I am Odysseus but I am also a siren,
calling for others to join me in the waves
though I dream of my feet in the sand,
misery loves company, or
maybe the lost just seek the lost
like blind poets seeking the light in a world made of nighttime.

I am Odysseus, but sometimes I am the lotus eater,
drunk on this place and this moment,
home forgotten in my moments of insobriety,
maybe this place can be enough
sometimes.

I am Odysseus, but sometimes I am Penelope,
waiting for someone to return home to me,
someone gone so long that I won't even recognize him
when I see him,
I seek comfort and isolation because accepting they aren't coming
home
feels like failure,
even though we all know the same man can't come home again.

I am Odysseus, sometimes monster, sometimes man, sometimes
hero.
I am lost and I am seeking, and I am homesick and I am moored in this
darkness.
This odyssey of mine is one of juxtaposition, dichotomy, oxymoron,
impossibilities made possible,
but then maybe this odyssey belongs to all of us.

Saturday Night Storm

water rises, rushes
drowns out who I was before
leaving only shadows

Starlight, Starbright

Eyes closed, Louisiana night all around us like warm bathwater,

"Are you wishing on that star?"

That single star above us, the only one shining beyond the city lights, the closest I can get to the rest of the universe without driving a few hours away,

I lie.

"No."

The future I'd dreamed inside my head fades away as I open my eyes, dreams of seeing the world with you, swimming in distant seas and climbing faraway mountains, wearing the dress and the ring, the crib, the laugh lines, the dream of *us* rises up into the darkness like a phantom and fades into oblivion, leaving only the dance of the starlight as proof it ever existed.

And I'm left to wonder how an entire life can disappear without even a whisper?

Tillandsia Usneoides

Clinging, climbing, choking.

He is stunted while you flourish. Parasite, you need him to survive. Whispers in the wind. You tell him that he needs you too. He listens to your song until he believes the lies. He tries not to notice when you steal his sunlight.

The world watches you in awe; you are a tourist destination. The Yankees come and take your picture without a thought to your host. He is the wall that holds the Mona Lisa, a necessity but never a desire. And while you may not kill him quickly (you are a slow cancer not a bullet wound)—while he may live a long and healthy life—one day a storm will blow in, and when he tries to bend to Gaia's will, he will find you rigid. Arms splayed out, he will crack against the wind, fall in hopes you'll catch him.

But you won't be there.

While his lifeblood bleeds out over his broken body, you will inch away in search of another lover, another victim for your selfish, beautiful game.

Red Polo

I watch you slip through the TSA,
  your red polo shirt clean and bright
from its time in my washer machine,
and I realize that I'll never see you wearing that shirt again,
I'll never see you wave to me again,
I'll never see you push your glasses further up your nose again—
I am watching you walk out of my life
and you don't even know it.

How Many Words?

We sit next to one another on the patio we added to the house after we bought it. I drape my legs over yours while the dogs play in the yard. It's hot, but then again, it's always hot. The soft fabric of my shirt clings to my back, but I can barely feel it with my skin touching yours the way that it is, my hand holding yours. It's just a Sunday morning. There is no jazz in the streets this early, no po boys to be eaten, no parades to watch. This is not a moment of beautiful New-Orleans-colored bliss, this is just bliss. Me and you, you and me—bliss, that kind of bliss. A simple Sunday morning with you near me, you with me, you on the same page as me. And when I open my eyes and this rose-colored dream starts to slip away, I reach out and hold it for a moment, for two moments, for three moments of a happiness I fear I may never know, a happiness I fear we may never know. There are 1,000 miles between us, but two simple words would close the distance: "I'm moving." Or maybe three words: "I choose you." Or maybe fourteen words: "After all the years you've been waiting, I'm ready to be with just you." The exact words don't matter. All that I'll remember when it's over is that you wanted me or that you didn't, that you chose a life of Sunday mornings or you didn't. That you're here or you're not.

Little Boy Laughter

laughter rings out down the hall,
 my laughter always loudest, then yours, then his
Daddy is so silly, mama.□
I always thought he'd sound like you,
but he sounds like my brother at five years old,
a memory of a memory

four dogs, one always under foot,
fur all over this house we call a home
there are dog toys and toy trains all over the floor,
he likes trains because his pepé drives trains
and one day his pepé promises he'll drive him around on the engine

Mardi Gras beads pile up in the closet
he loves Carnival,
he says the rest of the year is simply waiting for the parades and the
King Cake

he grows up in a world we created for him,
a world of books and computers,
my world and yours,
we place bets on whether he'll be a writer or a computer engineer
and we both share our passions with him
without realizing that he'll be someone like and unlike us both
a person all his own,
no matter how many bets we place

and at night we sleep beneath an old roof,
a roof from a world so unlike our own
they wouldn't believe in us if someone showed them a window to the
future,
their hard work has become our safe haven,
has become my dream,
a dream of a world full of
little boy laughter,
dog fur,
toy trains,
colorful beads,
dreams
and us,
most importantly, dreams of us

A Goodbye Song

Standing on the banks of the bayou, wondering how it will feel to live in a place without bayous. Can some new place be home if this place is still home? Watery summers, heavy air, weekends filled with saxophones and trumpets and trashcan drums, dancing until my legs ache, beignets and crawfish boils, late night art markets and art making, a celebration of living. Dear New Orleans Sunset, tell me: how can any place but here be home?

in some other place,
some other reality,
I refuse to leave,
I don't pack the U-Haul
I take root like Spanish moss—
□*I stay.*

The Right Questions

Is one lost if she's
merely
searching for the right questions
to ask?

Small Lies

At first, we don't talk about the future.

We live in this moment, in the laughter in this loud bar, in the shitty cover band destroying Ed Sheeran songs, and the love building in both of us like a summer storm. When the clouds come, we wait them out. We stay indoors and drink sweet tea. And then we talk about the future like it's the plot of a romance novel, not the reality of two people building a life together.

We talk about Florida and New York City. You tell me you could put down roots in the Village if I sold enough poems to buy you a private jet for weekend getaways to Orlando. I tell you private jets are bad for the environment, but maybe we could work something out. We talk about pasta and art in Italy and romance and wine in Paris. We make a movie trailer of the highlights of our life together and watch it whenever doubt sets in.

We carefully avoid the rift forming between us, the chasm of incompatibility in the form of a single disagreement, a crucial point of opposition.

I don't ever want to be someone's mother, you say.

But I do, I say.

We spend the rest of the drive home from the airport in the comfort of small lies. We promise to stay friends, agree that this was the most civil break-up we've ever gone through, and swallow the tears until there's more distance between us. I cry all the way home, and I think about how odd it is to give up one living, breathing, beautiful human for a tiny human who doesn't even exist yet, but still, it feels like "the right thing to do."

Whatever that means.

The Savannah

he watches me from the shade of a baobab tree

he sees the scars on my back, the anger and the hurt in my yellow
eyes—

he knows I am no prize, no trophy pelt to hang on a wall

he doesn't even consider shooting sleep into my veins and slipping me
into a cage,

so he waits for me to tire of the savannah,

patiently

he waits for me to come to him and share secrets with my lips,

but he never tries to keep me, he loves me when my legs carry me back
to him,

and he loves me when they carry me away again

he sees the scars from the man who tried to tame me,

the man who tried to break me with a collar and the promise of a
comfortable life—

and he promised himself he would rather love a wild woman in the
parts and the moments I can spare

(wild women are also so busy, there is so much to be done, so many things to change)□

than smother the fire in my eyes with domestication

wild things deserve the open savannah, the hunt, the whole world

and he's not the sort to deny me anything

Stay

You make me want to stay still and that scares me because I'm the girl who never stops. I am always going, always running from this moment to the next. I moved 1,000 miles away on a whim, and I danced in the streets and caught beads with a heart full of living. I don't know how to be satisfied, but sometimes when I am lying next to you, I imagine a future without New-York-City colored dreams. I think of buying a house with a yard instead of renting an apartment in the center of the universe.

Pause—

I think of *buying a house*, something I've spent my entire adult life swearing I'd never do. When someone asked when I was going to settle down, I'd smile and tell them I'm not the settling down type. I am a runner, a dreamer, a woman with fully functional wings, and I soar above all the people who settled down, laughing, because I never make it to the "let's build a life together" stage.

Life and love are so fleeting and staying still feels like giving up, like it's the death of the person I've been my entire life—but with you, with you, I think that maybe I could stay and not die. I could stay and still fly. I could have a house and children and a Subaru (never a minivan), and I could be content.

Content—there's a word I never thought I'd use to describe myself. I convinced myself that an inability to be content meant I'd always be reaching, always be climbing to a summit no one had ever seen before, instead of facing the trauma and fears of mediocrity that plagued me. Where I come from, people don't get to live the life I've lived, and I have spent my life defying everyone's low expectations. And I never ever thought I'd be here with you, a boy from the very same desolate place I come from, falling in love and thinking about sitting still. But here we are, two people with a new future coming into focus through the camera lens, a family portrait with a woman who somehow became her mother and a question hanging between us

— *how did we get here and why didn't we get here sooner?*

Spoken word poem, first aired on WHRO Public Media, Writer's Block Radio Show

Love You Like

I don't love you like a storm or a hurricane
the windows don't shake and the earth doesn't split open because I
love you
no volcanic eruptions or other natural disasters need referencing to
explain how I feel.

I don't love you like a fire burning a house to the ground
buildings don't crumble and cities don't fall because I love you
I can breathe when we are apart,
my heart keeps beating, blood keeps pumping through my veins
I could live without you, but I just don't want to.

I love you like a warm fireplace and a heavy blanket
like the spider's web thriving in the corner of our front porch,
stronger than anything manmade but still delicate and beautiful,
familiar, not dangerous.

I love you like the smell of hot chocolate
like the softness of a pillow after a long day
you are soft pastels and a Monet painting (never a Picasso or a Dali)
warm water lilies and the serenity of a pond we want to put in our
backyard
next to the chicken coop I swear we'll have one day

I love you like spring and autumn,
like rereading the same book because I want to
not because it's my only choice.

I love you like home because you are my home
you are the windows and foundation,
the peeling paint and the hardwood floors,
the memories and the love that cling to the walls like fresh wallpaper.

I love you like the afternoon we spent walking around our neighbor-
hood
talking softly while the baby slept in her pram,
making plans for the rest of our lives together.

I love you like safety and gentleness, like promises and goodnight
kisses,
like the bees love the flowers and ducks love the rain.

The thing is—I have loved burning infernos and category fives
and they left the kind of destruction that took years to rebuild
my days of storm chasing have exhausted me
and that's not the life I want

Our love wasn't written in the stars
(is any love truly fated)
but I *choose* you
and for me, that's more important than fate.

Gylou

you built a graveyard in my womb
the least you could do is leave flowers

Edges

I am all sharp edges
The furniture you bang your knee on
In the middle of the night
The *goddammit* that slips out
In frustration and pain
The throbbing that continues into the morning
A reminder of the night that will not end

I am all sharp edges
The blade that slices your skin
Stinging as the bite of the fruit
Mixes with your blood
Layers of frustration and discomfort,
A siren that screams for you to feel her
Acknowledge her

I am all sharp edges

Metal and glass

Paper and thorns–

Everything that hurts

When pressed against delicate skin

I am the darkness and the blade

The forgetting and the remembering

An echo of what was lost when the leaves started to fall

I am something wild and angry

But I don't want to be–

I want to believe that I get to come back from this,

That I can be rounded and softened

Filed into something beautiful, not dangerous

October

Skeletons of leaves crunch across a porcelain floor
thickest of shadows in the darkest of autumn nights
graveyards of unmarked, empty graves
silence that does not give
when you press your palms against it

A late season hurricane with unforgiving waters
wind that is unafraid of what comes next
because there is no tomorrow when you are nature

Does anything ever end or is everything always ending?

A dawn swallows the night that birthed Her
fighting against the goddamn stars that always come
devouring what could have been
creating a new world with her might,
with her indignation

A monster made of more than claws and teeth
because living beyond *this* is the fury unrelenting,
The starving grief, swallowing and swallowing
consuming and consuming
tearing with teeth made of the longest night
eating even the bones and the memory
of the time I asked my 7th grade science teacher
Where is the soul? when she described the anatomy
of the great apes

I used to love October
but now I'd like to scrub her from human history
until my elbows break

Wraith Like Me

Blackness that does not awaken
 when the sun screeches its song across the morning
heavy like the weight of too many blankets
huddled under too many bodies
there were poppies once
lace, too
but never velvet because I'm allergic
forget-me-nots on a glow-in-the-dark dinosaur comforter
there might have been magic
but magic never lingers once the moon is swallowed
face red
hands soft, still-forgiving
freckles that burned in the summertime
beacons of a place you've never seen
something other than the night
but the napalm in my veins left nothing
nothing

I have tried to peel back the night
to pull the stars apart with my teeth
but the morning frost never comes
it is always autumn and I am always dying
winter, spring, summer never come
and I'm sorry you've watched me choke to death
every night since the river broke
and all that is left,
all that remains–
I used to come alive in springtime
but now She'll never come

October 2.0

October 2021

a spark
a light without sound
three ultrasounds
and no rhythm, no beat
a loss my body missed,
hoping that reality could be altered
a song could begin
but everything remains
silent
gone
a child lost

October 2022

another child,
seventeen
a reminder that hurt children

hurt people
a castle of lies is raised to the ground
like so many cards
a fire catches
smolders
then goes out
a child broken

October exists to remind us we were allotted one child,
one wild wonderful child who is *enough*
who will always be enough.

A lesson I received,
internalized,
understood.

I don't believe in god
but I believe in the power of October.

Lego Mansions

I watch you build a mansion out of Legos
flowers sprout from the roof
and there are pools in every room
it's nonsensical in the way
that a four-year-old's mansion would be
nonsensical and beautiful and strange
a reflection of all the parts of me
I hoped you'd inherit,
in a world so full of black and white
you are a kaleidoscope–
and I remember,
I remember the times
there were only a few, but there were times□
when I thought monochrome
was the world entirely
that the color had been drained from the palette
and all the flowers and the pools weren't worth

staying for
I remember the times when it felt like
too much
to continue waking up to the blinding sun
in a world so full of
blades and bullets and barbed wire,
all the times that came so close
to a world without your Lego mansions,
your paintings hanging on every wall of our house,
your father's eyes, my nose–
imagining a world without you
is so much darker
than imagining a world without me
and I say a few *thank you*s to the girl
in the dark who put one foot in front of the other and
stayed

Author's Afterword

Sharing my lived experience was difficult. It was vulnerable and scary. Putting it out in the world was something I have hesitated to do for a long time, but now it's out there and I hope it helps someone somewhere feel less alone. What I know is that women in this world are far more likely to experience violence and trauma at the hands of men than not. I know that what I lived through has marked me. It governs all my interactions with the world, and I know that many women share that with me. I wish we didn't. I wish we weren't all in this sisterhood together, but here we are.

I hope that if anyone is reading this collection who has the ability to be a source of positive change in this world (to include: mothers, fathers, teachers, counselors—pretty much anyone who has the ability to help raise a generation of boys who come into adulthood more softly) takes their responsibility very seriously. I want my daughter to live in a different reality than I do. I want better for her. It is the greatest hope of my life, the deepest desire of my life—to save her from my experiences. Please help me with that, if you can.

Thank you for going on this journey with me. It was a tough one to put together and finally release, but I trust all of your with my words, my memories, my life.

Coming Soon

RISE OF THE
Witch Queen

RIFT OF REALMS
BOOK ONE

GENEVA OLEANDER